MUSIC IC

R&B AND RAP COLORING BOOK
(UNOFFICIAL)

ADULT COLOR THERAPY

M. CRYPTKEEPER

ISBN: 1546606858

ISBN-13: 978-1546606857

INTRODUCTION

COLOR YOUR FAVORITE MUSIC ARTISTS INCLUDING: ASAP ROCKY, CHANCE THE RAPPER, DRAKE, CHILDISH GAMBINO, GUCCI MANE, KANYE WEST, THE WEEKND, KENDRICK LAMAR, TYLER THE CREATOR AND XXX TENTATION.

PERFECT WHEN ACCOMPANIED WITH A MATCHING SPOTIFY PLAYLIST OR ALBUM.

EACH PAGE IS DOUBLED SO YOU'LL BE ABLE TO KEEP AN ORIGINAL OUTLINE TO SCAN COPY FOR FUTURE COLORING USE.

HAND DRAWN ILLUSTRATIONS BY M. CRYPTKEEPER

CONTENTS

WHAT IS RAPPING AND R&B?

RAPPING, RHYMING, SPITTING AND MCING

IS A POPULAR MUSICAL FORM OF VOCAL DELIVERY. THIS INCORPORATES: RHYME, RHYTHMIC SPEECH AND STREET LANGUAGE (SLANG).
THIS IS THEN PERFORMED IN A VARIETY OF WAYS, COMMONLY OVER A BACKBEAT.

THE KEY COMPONENTS OF RAP INCLUDE:

- CONTENT SUBJECT MATTER.
- FLOW (THE RHYTHM AND RHYME).
- DELIVERY (HOW THE PIECE IS SPOKEN THROUGH TONE AND EMOTION).

RAP IS OFTEN ASSOCIATED WITH HIP-HOP MUSIC. HOWEVER RAP'S ORIGINS PREDATE THE HIP-HOP CULTURE.

R&B IS SHORT FOR: RHYTHM AND BLUES.

R&B IS A TYPE OF POP MUSIC WITH BLACK ORIGIN. IT HAS A SOULFUL VOCAL STYLE PAIRED WITH A BACKTRACK (OR DONE ACAPELLA).

This page has been kept blank to prevent pen **BLEEDING.**

This page has been kept blank to prevent pen BLEEDING.

3

CHANCE THE TRAPPER

This page has been kept blank to prevent pen **BLEEDING.**

3

CHANCE THE TRAPPER

This page has been kept blank to prevent pen **BLEEDING.**

DRAKE

I know when that hotline bling That can only mean one thing

You only live once

I got enemies, got a lotta enemies. Got a lotta people tryna drain me of my energy

This page has been kept blank to prevent pen **BLEEDING**.

DRAKE

I know when that hotline bling
That can only mean one thing

You only live once

I got enemies,
got a lotta enemies. Got a lotta
people tryna drain me of my energy

This page has been kept blank to prevent pen BLEEDING.

This page has been kept blank to prevent pen BLEEDING.

This page has been kept blank to prevent pen **BLEEDING.**

This page has been kept blank to prevent pen BLEEDING.

This page has been kept blank to prevent pen BLEEDING.

KANYE'S.

I am a god

I love you like Kanye loves Kanye

One good girl
s worth a thousand bitches

This page has been kept blank to prevent pen **BLEEDING.**

KANYE WEST

I am a god

I love you like Kanye loves Kanye

One good girl is worth a thousand bitches

This page has been kept blank to prevent pen **BLEEDING.**

This page has been kept blank to prevent pen BLEEDING.

This page has been kept blank to prevent pen **BLEEDING.**

Loyalty, got royalty inside my DNA

Sit Down, Be Humble.

"Girl, I'm Kendrick Lamar"

This page has been kept blank to prevent pen **BLEEDING.**

Loyalty, got royalty inside my DNA

Sit Down, Be Humble. @

"Girl, I'm Kendrick Lamar"

This page has been kept blank to prevent pen **BLEEDING.**

This page has been kept blank to prevent pen **BLEEDING.**

This page has been kept blank to prevent pen **BLEEDING.**

This page has been kept blank to prevent pen BLEEDING.

This page has been kept blank to prevent pen BLEEDING.

THANK YOU FOR SUPPORTING PUMPKIN PUBLICATIONS, I HOPE YOU'RE NOT TOO SPOOKED.

PLEASE LEAVE A REVIEW IF POSSIBLE, AS YOUR FEEDBACK IS MUCH APPRECIATED.

ABOUT THE AUTHOR

M. CRYPTKEEPER IS A GRADUATED ART STUDENT BASED IN THE UNITED KINGDOM (LONDON ESSEX). WITH A PASSION FOR ILLUSTRATION AND HORROR IT ONLY MADE SENSE FOR HER TO START PUMPKIN PUBLICATIONS: AN INDIE BOOK COMPANY THAT SPECIALIZES IN MODERN HORROR FOLK TALES AND HAND DRAWN COLOUR THERAPY. HER QUIRKY STYLE INSTANTLY TRANSLATES INTO HER BOOKS CREATING A TRULY IMMERSIVE EXPERIENCE.

Made in the USA
Coppell, TX
16 December 2020

45310678R10031